VARSITY
AND
HOAXES

F.A. REEVE

THE OLEANDER PRESS OF CAMBRIDGE

The Oleander Press
17 Stansgate Avenue
Cambridge CB2 2QZ

ISBN 0 900891 16 5

British Library Cataloguing in Publication Data

Reeve, Frank Albert
    Varsity rags and hoaxes. — (Cambridge town, gown
    and county; vol. 17).
    1. University of Cambridge — Students 2. Student
    activities — England — Cambridge
    I. Title II. Series
    378'.1'98'9   LF 529

Designed by Ron Jones

Printed and bound by The Burlington Press, Foxton

CONTENTS

  I Wigs on the statues on Trinity College Library 5
 II Students impersonate gypsies 5
III A nightwatchman and his hut pitched into the river . . . 7
 IV Zachariah Whitmore's water velocipede 7
  V Charlie Carter visits his old Eton gentlemen 8
 VI Baiting the police 8
VII Bishop Selwyn's dive 10
VIII Calverley steals a sign 10
 IX The windows of King's College Chapel removed in two
    nights 12
  X The Shah of Persia Hoax, 1873 14
 XI The voting on degrees for women, 1897 15
XII Lord Kitchener mobbed, 1898 18
XIII The Sultan of Zanzibar Hoax, 1905 19
XIV No breakfast with the Master 23
 XV The attempt to kidnap Keir Hardie 24
XVI The Haddock Hoax 26
XVII Guy Fawkes celebrations 26
XVIII Impersonating Carry Nation 27
XIX The attempt to seize Sir Norman Angell 29
 XX Mock funerals 30
XXI The Emmanuel College Insurance Society 31
XXII The Pavement Club 34
XXIII Sir Arthur Conan Doyle fails to materialise 35
XXIV The opening of Toot-an-kum-in's tomb 37
XXV The unveiling of Eros by King Henry VIII 38
XXVI The opening of Joanna Southcott's box 39
XXVII Night Climbers 39
XXVIII Climbing King's College Chapel 41
XXIX Poppy day 42
XXX The best undergraduate prank of all time? 47

Note on H.A. Moden and F. Keene

At the turn of the century, a series of amusing sketches by Harry A. Moden and Frank Keene commenting upon Town and Gown life were published by the Cambridge Picture Postcard Company and sold for one penny. The main series was called *University Sketches,* and other cards depicted local events such as the passing of the horse trams and the Sultan of Zanzibar hoax. A set of four depicted *Recreation* (a student setting off for a country walk with a young lady); *Flirtation* (the couple seated at a quiet spot); *Consternation* (on the arrival of a proctor and his bulldogs); and *Botheration* (the young man having his name taken).

*Photographs 2,3,4,6,8,11 and 12 are reproduced by
courtesy of the Cambridge and County Folk Museum and
the front cover illustration by courtesy of the
Cambridgeshire Collection, Cambridgeshire Libraries.
The other plates are from the author's collection.*

VARSITY RAGS
AND
HOAXES

I. WIGS ON THE STATUES ON TRINITY COLLEGE LIBRARY

George Pryme, who was born in 1781 and died at the age of 87, was one of the first members of the university to take an interest in town affairs and was known as Counsellor Pryme. He became a Fellow of Trinity, the first Professor of Political Economy in any British university, and was M.P. for Cambridge in 1832, 1835 and 1837.

In his *Autobiographical Recollections,* Pryme says that twenty years before his time the senior Fellows of Trinity wore wigs, and there was a barber's shop just within the gate near Bishop's Hostel where Fellows were powdered and their wigs dressed. One Saturday night, when the barber was dressing the Sunday wigs, he was bribed to give them up to some practical jokers who climbed to the parapet of the Library and placed them on the heads of the four statues facing the Hall.

On Sunday, the seniors were distressed to find that their best wigs were missing, and had to go to dinner, then held during the morning, in their old wigs. When they came out of Hall into Nevile's Court and looked up, they saw them on the statues. Pryme adds that the identity of the practical jokers was never discovered.

II. STUDENTS IMPERSONATE GYPSIES

The *Cambridge Chronicle* relates how in 1805, two students made a bet of £500 that they would dress as gypsies and, carrying earthenware, ride unmolested on asses from Cambridge to Tottenham. They accomplished this feat successfully, but on the return journey they entered a wood near the town and made a fire to cook some food. They were apprehended by a farmer and taken before the magistrates, but were released when they told their story.

1. The Police Make an Arrest! (F. Keene)

III. A NIGHT WATCHMAN AND HIS HUT PITCHED INTO THE RIVER

One undergraduate prank enabled a poor Cambridge boy to begin what became a prosperous career. Three Fellow-Commoners from Trinity College and one from Jesus College obtained some of the strong Trinity audit ale, so-called because this special brew was offered to tenants when they called to pay their rents. The undergraduates went to the hut of a night watchman in King Street, and gave him so much ale that he fell asleep. They then picked up the hut with the man inside, and pitched it into the river.

When the college authorities learned about this exploit, the men were gated for the rest of the term and ordered to copy out 500 lines of Ovid. A young man named Rowe, who was a good penman, heard about this and offered to write the lines for them. His grandfather had come to Cambridge from Cornwall in 1740 and had begun to grow vegetables at Paradise Garden at Newnham. While the young man's father was building a house at the garden, unfavourable weather caused him to get into debt, and he was imprisoned in the castle. His son had to survive by begging for food and hawking vegetables in the streets, while Mrs Soward, cowkeeper at Newnham, gave him a bed.

The undergraduates accepted his offer to write their lines, and young Rowe sat up all night to complete the task. He did it so well that they gave him enough money to free his father from the castle, and the Jesus man became so interested in him that he obtained for him the post of private secretary to the tutor of his college.

Rowe later had several other posts in the university; he learned Latin and French, and became an alderman of the Town Council. He bought the estate of Mrs Soward, who had befriended him, and helped her son when he was in need. He died at the age of 81 in 1878.

IV. ZACHARIAH WHITMORE'S WATER VELOCIPEDE

On the 29th May, 1822, the following notice was displayed in several places in Cambridge:

'Zachariah Whitmore of Philadelphia, North America, begs to inform the inhabitants of Cambridge that he intends starting from Lynn on his Water Velocipede at 12 o'clock, and will arrive at Cambridge between 6 and 7 o'clock in the evening on Whit Monday next!'

About two thousand people waited for several hours before they concluded that they had been hoaxed.

V.   CHARLIE CARTER VISITS HIS OLD ETON GENTLEMEN

The Rev. H.I.C. Blake, in *The Cantab,* published in 1845, relates how Charlie Carter, who was employed at Eton College, came to Cambridge to try to recover money due to him from some former scholars. He went to King's College, which at that time had 60 Fellows but only 10 scholars, dressed in a white hat, peagreen coat, white waistcoat, inexpressibles and top boots. While they dined in Hall, the scholars left him in charge of the college cook. Harry Matthews suggested that they should give a wine party and invite Charlie, give him plenty of drink, and then sew him up and send him back to Eton by the mail coach.

Charlie, who had been sampling the strong beer in the Buttery Hatch, at once accepted Matthew's invitation to take a glass of wine or two in his rooms, when they would come to a settlement regarding his long-outstanding bills for the use of boats and guns. After Charlie had been well primed with wine, he was sewn up in an old greatcoat by the bedmaker and taken to the mail coach office. A label was fastened to his back, and the guard was bribed to ensure that when they reached London, he would be safely delivered to Eton by the Windsor coach.

It is said that Charlie never troubled the scholars again.

VI.   BAITING THE POLICE

Generations of students have attempted to obtain a policeman's helmet to hang up in their room. In the autumn of 1858 there were frequent affrays between university boating-men and the police, and Mr Balls, the Mayor, had to try many cases of assault and battery. Police officer 'K.' was especially disliked and he was the subject of a rhyme: 'If policeman K. arrests you, let not your spirits damp; Break his head and

PROGGINS!! *Varsity Sketches, No. 54.*
"**Proctor & Bulldogs.**"

HAModen

2. Proctor and Bulldogs (H.A. Moden)

shave his whiskers, and suspend him to a lamp!'

The officer in question unwisely entered the Great Court of Trinity on the night of the First Trinity Boat Club supper, and he was so maltreated that some of the offenders were arrested and later imprisoned.

VII. BISHOP SELWYN'S DIVE

One would hardly suppose that Bishop Selwyn, one of the great ecclesiastical figures of the nineteenth century, would have been the perpetrator of a hoax. George Augustus Selwyn, born in 1809, became the first Bishop of New Zealand and later of Lichfield. Immediately after his death, it was decided to establish a college in Cambridge which would bear his name.

During a visit to Heidelberg, when he was a young man, he noticed that the swimming-bath used by the German students was connected with the river by a short tunnel which could be entered. He dived into the bath and went through the tunnel to the river, while the spectators anxiously waited for him to reappear. After five minutes, when they were preparing to search for his body, he returned through the tunnel, and to the amazement of the German students, rose to the surface with a pebble in his hand.

VIII. CALVERLEY STEALS A SIGN

The poet Calverley was a high-spirited young man who had already been sent down from Oxford before he entered Christ's College. A bronze plaque with the text of his *Ode to Tobacco,* written while he was at college in 1862, may be seen affixed to the wall of Bacon's shop at the corner of Rose Crescent. He had a great reputation for making daring leaps, and once jumped over a horse in Green Street wearing his cap and gown and with his hands in his pockets.

One day he stole the sign of the *Green Man* public house at Trumpington, and ran back to Christ's College, pursued by the landlord and others. When he reached the college, he ordered the porter to close the

"RAGTIME" IN CAMBRIDGE.

3. "Ragtime" in Cambridge (H.A. Moden)

gate, hid the sign under his bed, and then returned to the court to join men who had been attracted by the clamour outside.

The Dean appeared and wanted to know what the trouble was, and Calverley remarked that the men outside sought a sign, but none could be given them, evidently a reference to a passage in the Gospel of St. Matthew, "An evil and adulterous generation seeketh after a sign; and there shall no sign be given it."

One day, when Calverley was walking across the sacred lawn of King's College, he met the Provost and was sternly rebuked. As Calverley did not seem to be very impressed, the Provost exclaimed, "Do you know who I am?" "No" said Calverley. "Look again, sir, and tell me what you see before you." Calverley quietly remarked, "I see an elderly gentleman, apparently very irascible."

11

IX. THE WINDOWS OF KING'S COLLEGE CHAPEL REMOVED IN TWO NIGHTS

Visitors to King's College Chapel often ask how the windows escaped destruction during the Civil War, when bands of soldiers drilled and exercised in the Chapel, and William Dowsing was smashing windows and statues elsewhere.

The noted Cambridge antiquary Cole, who had rooms in King's in 1735, wrote: "There is a tradition that this (the West window which until 1879 was filled with plain glass) was broken by soldiers in the Rebellion, upon which the rest were taken down and hidden under the organ loft. If it is true, there is such a place big enough to hold them, but I am well informed that they have never been removed, except for repairs, but it is a wonder that, being so beautiful and regular, they were spared by the enemies of such beauty."

Following the publication in 1854 of a book entitled *The Chorister, a Tale of King's College Chapel in the Civil Wars,* by the Rev. S. Baring-Gould of Clare College, a prolific writer of abstruse works, novels and folk-tales, many people firmly believed that all of the windows had been taken out and buried.

The book describes how, in 1637, James Fleetwood, a Fellow of King's, and William the Chorister made plans for the safety of the windows.

"The darkness of night was settling in, but no one had remarked that several ladders were fixed against the south side of King's College Chapel, few heard any sound, yet the great windows were being stripped of their stained glass, piecemeal, by Waltheram the glass manufacturer and about eight scholars of the college; and as fast as the glass was taken down, several of the boys of the choir packed in it hampers which Fleetwood and William carried off and buried in the garden where during the day pits had been dug. In this manner they proceeded rapidly, and when morning dawned the east and the whole range of the south window frames and casements were glassless."

"It was night again . . . the last windows of the Chapel were being removed, and several were to be buried beneath the pavement of the Chapel . . . Morning came again, and with it came the talking, gaping

12

4. After the Rag: reviewing the force (H.A. Moden)

people, thronging about the Chapel, and wondering to see all of the stained glass windows had gone."

Towards the end of the book we learn that William was brought before Cromwell, condemned and shot before the altar, in his stainless white robes, because he had refused to confess where the windows had been hidden. And at Grantchester "beneath the shadow of the ivy mantled old church, sleeps the chorister." There was an illustration of Grantchester Church, and towards the end of the nineteenth century many people remembered having had the alleged tombstone of the chorister pointed out to them.

James Fleetwood was admitted as a Scholar in 1622 and succeeded Provost Whichcote in 1660. Between 1854 and 1895, ten editions of the book were published, so it is not surprising that the story became widely known.

The author had stated that his book was based on information given in Treumann's *Notices of Collegiate Buildings,* and when, in 1899, the Rev. E.G. Swain wrote to enquire about this work, which he had been unable to trace, he received the following reply, now in the University Library:

Dear Sir,

     'The Chorister' was written 9 March 1854 and was really a hoax played on some friends, fellow under-grads. The reference to authority was to an author who never existed. It was a silly production which I trusted had been forgotten long ago.

Yours Truly,
S. Baring-Gould

N. Devon
June 28, 1899."

X.   THE SHAH OF PERSIA HOAX, 1873

The perpetrators of this famous hoax remained unknown, and it was thought that townsmen, rather than undergraduates, may have been responsible.

    The Shah of Persia was in England at the time, and a telegram, purporting to come from Crewe, where he was staying, was handed to the Mayor. It stated that His Excellency intended to visit Cambridge.

    His Worship promptly informed the members of the Corporation and the Vice-Chancellor. Hasty arrangements were made for a luncheon, the Volunteers were summoned by bugle, and representatives of the town and the University went to the railway station, the Mayor and Corporation in their robes, and preceded by mace bearers.

    The Town Clerk had written an address of welcome, expressing the pride felt by Cambridge in this visit. Just before the train was due, the platform was crowded with important people. In front was the Mayor, beside him the Town Clerk, also the Vice-Chancellor and other representatives of the university.

    The train arrived, but no Shah alighted, and the people on the platform realised that they had been hoaxed. Robes were discarded and taken back to the Guildhall in a brake, and the distinguished persons made their way homewards. The Volunteers boldly returned through the streets with their band playing.

In the evening, news reached Cambridge that the Shah had actually been attending a royal garden party. "Sam George" composed a song which was sold in the streets for one penny, and was sung for many years afterwards. Some of the verses are:

"Hark my friends, and hear what I say,
It was a lark on Saturday,
And all the people now do say,
    Have you seen the Shah of Persia?

It was reported he would come
To see the sights of Cambridge town;
But folks found out they had been done,
    About the Shah of Persia.

The horses from the "Bull" were got,
The postillions looked so very hot,
As up to the station fast they trot,
    To fetch the Shah of Persia.

The rifles too as quick as shot
Were also to the station got,
(The captain looked so devilish hot)
    To salute the Shah of Persia.

The Mayor and Council so queer did look,
As from the station they took their hook;
The tale will be told in many a book,
    About the Shah of Persia."

XI.   THE VOTING ON DEGREES FOR WOMEN, 1897

There were memorable scenes on 21 May 1897, when voting took place in the Senate House to decide whether women should be given degrees. Special trains came from London to bring M.A.s entitled to vote, and long before the doors of the Senate House were opened at

5. Senate House Hill, 1897, while voting was taking place to decide whether degrees should be awarded to women.

1 p.m., a huge crowd had assembled. Some people even climbed to the roof over the northern aisle of Great St. Mary's Church.

Many placards had been posted up: 'ENGLAND EXPECTS EVERY M.A.(N) TO DO HIS DUTY.' 'GET THEE TO GIRTON, BEATRICE, GET THEE TO NEWNHAM, THIS IS NO PLACE FOR YOU MAIDS.' 'NO WOMAN SHALL COME WITHIN A MILE OF MY COURTS.'

6. Bacon's shop on the following day. The men at the upper windows were glaziers repairing windows broken during the rag.

From the upper floors of the bookshop of Macmillan and Bowes at 1 Trinity Street, then a lodging-house for undergraduates, hung a large effigy of a female in bloomers and mounted on a bicycle. M.A.s waiting on the Senate House lawn for the result of the voting were bombarded with confetti, squibs and crackers.

Scenes of wild rejoicing greeted the result, announced soon after 3 p.m.: 1,707 against, 661 for. By 7 p.m. townsmen had joined the celebrating gownsmen, and the Market Square was crowded. There were spectators at every window above the shops, and fireworks, eggs and fruit were aimed at them. The effigy on a bicycle was put on top of a hansom cab and taken to Newnham College, but the authorities had locked the gates. Professor Sidgwick, who was living there with his wife, who was Vice-Principal and Bursar, came out and said "Gentlemen, I think you had better go home," and they dispersed. On the Market Square, a huge bonfire burned until midnight. Hoardings, shop shutters, 80 yards of fencing from the New Museums and more from Queens' College, even a brewer's dray, fed the bonfire. By the following morning, most of the rooms overlooking the Square had broken windows and walls stained by rotten eggs and fruit. Undergraduates later subscribed money to compensate the victims.

XII.   LORD KITCHENER MOBBED, 1898

Lord Kitchener, fresh from his successes in Egypt, visited Cambridge on 24 November 1898 to receive an Honorary Degree and the Freedom of the Borough. An enormous crowd of people surrounded the Senate House and so many of them pressed forward that a part of the railings gave way. When he emerged, the horses were taken out of his carriage and the shafts were manned by undergraduates. A triumphant procession slowly made its way to Christ's College, where he was to stay the night, but as the carriage was being dragged through the gateway, an axle caught against one side and the wheels collapsed. The crowd surged into the college, mobbing the Sirdar and fighting for pieces of the carriage as souvenirs.

In the evening he was due to go to the Union Society to be installed as an honorary member. His uniform had been damaged and the streets were so crowded that it seemed unwise to venture out, but his cousin, Mrs Peile, suggested that he should change into civilian clothes and go there by side streets. At the Union he remarked grimly: "I only wish I had had some of you with me in the Sudan," but the audience missed the sarcasm and cheered the remark.

Placards forbidding bonfires and fireworks had been posted up in the town, but soon after 8.00 p.m. a huge bonfire was made in the Market Square. The whole town was scoured for wood, and railings, shutters from shop windows and even the doors of houses were seized. A witness said that the scene was "more like hell than anything I know". As the hours passed, the pandemonium increased, and the bonfire raged until midnight.

XIII.   THE SULTAN OF ZANZIBAR HOAX, 1905

William Horace de Vere Cole was the instigator of so many hoaxes that he became known as the prince of practical jokers. One of his earliest and most famous exploits occurred in 1905 when he was an undergraduate at Trinity. He and his friend Adrian Stephen were sitting in his rooms one evening and feeling somewhat depressed, so they decided to plan something amusing.

The Sultan of Zanzibar was in England at the time, and Cole proposed that they should impersonate him and pay a state visit to Cambridge. They immediately thought of one difficulty; the Sultan's photograph had appeared in several newspapers, and he was not in the least like either of them, so they decided to represent his imaginary uncle, "Prince Muhason Ali."

They also reasoned that if they hoaxed the university authorities and their identities were subsequently discovered, they would be sent down, so they decided to hoax the Mayor instead.

The plan was carried out a few days later, and their version of what occurred was published later in a book written by Adrian Stephen. They recruited two Cambridge friends and another from Oxford, went to London, and were made up at a theatrical costumier's. After sending a telegram to the Mayor to announce their visit, they took the train back to Cambridge.

19

7. The Sultan of Zanzibar Hoax, 1905. From left to right: Adrian Stephen,
Bowen Colthurst, Horace Cole, Leland Buxton and "Drummer" Howard.

Their account says that they were met at the station by the Town Clerk, conveyed in a carriage to the Guildhall, and received by the Mayor. They first visited a charity bazaar being held in the Guildhall, and made purchases from all of the stalls. They were then shown round the principal colleges.

When it was time to end their visit, the Town Clerk accompanied them to the station. They did not of course wish to return to London, so when they reached the Great Eastern platform they hoisted up their robes and fled to what was then the entrance to the Great Northern part of the station. They jumped into hansom cabs and told the cabbies to drive away as quickly as possible into the country.

They left the cabs at a place where, by crossing fields, they could reach the house of a friend. There they discarded their costumes, had dinner, and went back to Trinity.

Cole wanted to publish their story, so he and Stephen went to London and called at the offices of the *Daily Mail.* The newspaper sent someone to Cambridge to confirm their claims, and published a full account of their exploit.

The identity of the hoaxers soon became known, and it was said that the Mayor asked the Vice-Chancellor to have them sent down. The Vice-Chancellor said that he would do so if the Mayor insisted, but he advised him that it would be better to let the matter drop. Most people thought that it had been an amusing exploit, and no action was taken against Cole and his friends.

The foregoing was taken from Adrian Stephen's version of the episode, and Horace Cole gave additional details, but it is necessary to add some comments. The Mayor knew about the earlier Shah of Persia hoax, and when the telegram arrived, both he and the Town Clerk realised that it might not be genuine. Accordingly, they decided not to make any extensive preparations. The carriage sent to meet the 'Prince' was not accompanied by the Town Clerk but by a waiter from the Lion Hotel, as it was thought probable that no one would arrive.

However, four gentlemen of dark complexion and wearing long white robes and turbans descended from the train, accompanied by "Mr. Lucas," who acted as interpreter. When they arrived at the Guild-hall, the Mayor was not entirely convinced that his visitors were the

8. The Cambridge Hoax. In Zanzibar. The latest! (F. Keene)

persons they represented themselves to be, but they played their parts so convincingly that they were treated with courtesy. There was only one brief moment of doubt when one of the visitors was heard to utter a four-letter word.

After visiting colleges for an hour, the Mayor and the Town Clerk said goodbye to their visitors on King's Parade.

Horace Cole, in an account of the hoax that he wrote later for a newspaper, said "We had invented a language of strange noises in the train, and I saluted with a wave of my hand and a loud "Aba sti lacka burga" a bust of Queen Victoria by Brock that was in the Guildhall, to the Mayor's evident delight." A police inspector who was given a shilling tip by the 'Prince' later made a special request to the Chief Constable that he should be allowed to retain the coin as a souvenir.

Cole and some friends, disguised as navvies, once roped off a large area of Piccadilly and began to tear up the roadway, but his most spectacular hoax was when he and friends impersonated the Emperor of Abyssinia and his suite, and visited H.M.S. Dreadnought, then lying off Weymouth. One member of his suite was Adrian Stephen's sister Virginia, later famous as Virginia Woolf, the novelist.

They were received on board by an admiral, and everything passed off smoothly, but when it became known that it was all a hoax, there were questions in the House of Commons. It was one thing to hoax the Mayor of Cambridge, a local tradesman, but quite another thing to fool an admiral and the Navy.

When Cole was married at a Chelsea Register Office in 1931 he took elaborate precautions against being victimised himself. He said "I've played 95 practical jokes in all parts of Europe and I have never been caught out. I did not intend to let anyone catch me this time."

§ Stephen, Adrian. *The "Dreadnought" Hoax.* London, Hogarth Press, 1936. This also describes the Sultan of Zanzibar hoax.

XIV.   NO BREAKFAST WITH THE MASTER

Several hoaxes at Trinity College were organized by a young man who later became an M.P. He issued invitations to all freshmen to have

9. Decorations on the Union during the 'Admission of Women' debate, October 1939. *(Cambridge Daily News)*

breakfast with the Master on a Sunday morning, and added that "Surplices will be worn." Unfortunately for the hoaxer, the Vice-Master discovered the plot and was able to warn everybody except two freshmen who managed to secure surplices and went to the Lodge, but they were not given breakfast.

The same man sent notices to all freshmen to ask them to assemble on the Backs at a stated time for a freshmen's photograph. He arrived with a tiny camera from a doll's house, and had a punt ready so that he could escape across the river if the crowd became threatening, but no one seemed to realise that it was a hoax.

XV.   THE ATTEMPT TO KIDNAP KEIR HARDIE

Keir Hardie, the Scottish miner who was an outstanding figure in the early days of the Labour Party, visited Cambridge to speak in the Guildhall. The promoters learned that some rowing men were plotting

10. A Bicycle on the Divinity School, 1942. *(Cambridge Daily News)*

to kidnap him and keep him locked up while the meeting was due to take place. They foiled the plot by disguising a man to resemble Hardie, met him at the station and drove him to the Great Gate of Trinity. The real Keir Hardie was met and taken secretly to King's until it was time to go to the Guildhall.

When the fake Keir Hardie arrived at Trinity, the plotters soon discovered that they had been deceived, and proceeded to damage the cab, then went to the Guildhall, where benches and windows were smashed, and eggs and other missiles were thrown at the speaker. He was eventually safely smuggled into King's. It was this visit of Keir Hardie that brought Hugh Dalton, later Lord Dalton, M.P. for Cambridge and Chancellor of the Exchequer, then an undergraduate at King's, into the Socialist Movement.

XVI. THE HADDOCK HOAX

Miles Malleson, the actor and dramatist, during his undergraduate days at Emmanuel College, had himself made-up by Willy Clarkson to resemble an elderly Member of Parliament named Haddock. He arrived in Cambridge from London, dined with the Master of his college, and later gave a lecture opposing Votes for Women. The lecture was fully reported in the *Cambridge Daily News* on the following day. The only other man in the secret was Norman Birkett, later Sir Norman Birkett K.C., who at the time was President of the Union.

XVII. GUY FAWKES CELEBRATIONS

Until recent years, huge crowds assembled in the centre of the city on the evenings of November 5th and Armistice Day. The market stalls were removed during the afternoon and police reinforcements, some mounted, were brought into the town. There was usually a bonfire, numerous fireworks thrown into the crowd, and attempts to extinguish all of the gas lamps. One of the most spectacular sights that I can recall was a blazing four-wheeler being dragged through the narrow Petty Cury.

To make the task of the police more difficult, a group of students would suddenly begin to run out of the Market Square, shouting "Up, up, up" and gathering reinforcements on the way to attack some more distant objective. In 1911, a crowd of 300 attempted to cross the Jesus Lock Bridge, but were thwarted by five policemen.

In 1912, there were celebrations on 4 and 6 November, because Guy Fawkes Day fell on a Sunday. Undergraduates broke into Newnham College and pulled up the hockey goalposts for a bonfire. The *Cambridge Independent Press* reported later that "It was rumoured that an attempt would be made to set light to the bandstand on Christ's Pieces — one policeman was overpowered by a party of undergraduates, and had his helmet stretched until it could be forced right over his head."

In 1920, both the New Theatre and the Police Station opposite were besieged after someone had suggested that "the Roberts should be put to bed and tucked up."

The celebrations took a more serious turn in 1948, when some university buildings which had gone through the war unscathed were severely damaged. An explosive charge broke seventy panes of ancient glass in the windows of the Senate House, did much damage to the interior, and the priceless windows of King's College Chapel only narrowly escaped destruction. Bricks were thrown through the windows of Newnham College, and several cars and a van belonging to a local tradesman were overturned and damaged.

Later, a fund was opened to reimburse the tradesman, not only to meet the cost of the repairs to his van, but because he was self-employed and had lost business while his vehicle was being repaired.

XVIII.   IMPERSONATING CARRY NATION

The photograph shows an undergraduate who impersonated Carry Nation when she was visiting Great Britain in 1908. If today we may say that Mary Whitehouse symbolises the campaign against permissiveness, Carry Nation became internationally famous as a temperance agitator.

Carry Amelia Moore Nation was born in the United States of America in 1846 and her first christian name is spelt Carry because it was written thus in the family Bible by her father, who was not very literate, although he was a successful stock-dealer and planter. He later lost most of his money. When Carry was still young, her mother began to have

11. An undergraduate impersonating Carry Nation, the
     American temperance reformer.

grandiose delusions that she was Queen Victoria, and spent the last three years of her life in the Missouri State Hospital for the Insane. Her mother's brother and sister were also insane.

Carry, nearly six feet tall and with extremely muscular arms, became very religious and claimed to have visions. When her first husband died of alcoholism, she became obsessed by the dangers of intemperance and organized a branch of the Woman's Christian Temperance Union in Kansas, one of the first states to adopt prohibition, although liquor could still be freely obtained at numerous 'joints'.

She and her supporters began to attack the saloons, not only smashing bottles of liquor, but also the furniture and fittings. In Spring 1900 her activities spread to other places with increasing violence. Her 'visions' convinced her that she was engaged in a divinely-inspired mission, and she maintained that the local prohibition laws entitled her, as a citizen, to attack anyone breaking the law. During the assaults on the saloons, her favourite weapon was a hatchet, and when she was arrested more than thirty times, the sales of small replicas of her hatchet helped to pay the fines.

She usually dressed in the black and white uniform of a deaconess. She had a ferocious temper, and when she was aroused it was said that she employed an amazingly vigorous invective in a King James version of Billingsgate speech. She was an unbalanced, ignorant and contentious woman of vast energies, and by the time that she toured the British Isles in 1908 her notoriety had become international. In this country she met with a very mixed reception and had little success, but in the U.S.A. she was the spearhead of those people who wanted to close down the saloons, and her campaign did much to bring about the Prohibition Act. She died in 1911.

XIX.   THE ATTEMPT TO SEIZE SIR NORMAN ANGELL

Many well-known men, when they have spoken in Cambridge, have received a rowdy reception from the students. It was anticipated that there would be trouble at a meeting to be addressed by Mr (later Sir) Norman Angell, as many of his audience would be ex-servicemen. His controversial book, *The Great Illusion,* had appeared in 1910, and had been published in seventeen other countries.

After the chairman and the first speaker had been barracked, the Proctor, Dr Glover, arrived in the hall. Someone began to switch off the lights one by one, until only a solitary light remained, and this was turned off and on. After one spell of darkness it was seen that the Proctor had been struck by a bag of flour, and was completely white.

He began by saying "Gentlemen, you have the advantage of me just now. You know what is annoying you, and I don't." He left after a few minutes, but there was pandemonium when Norman Angell rose to speak. Before long, the meeting was abandoned when it was learned that a naval undergraduate had fallen from an upstairs window and had been seriously injured.

A mob attempted to seize Mr Angell as he left the building, but he was rescued by the police and protected in the Fire Station until most of the demonstrators had dispersed. Some decided to follow a Boys' Brigade band that happened to pass, but others went to Merton Cottage, where he was thought to be staying, and pushed down thirty yards of wall.

XX.   MOCK FUNERALS

The most severe penalty that can be inflicted on an undergraduate for a serious offence against university or college regulations is to be "sent down" or obliged to leave Cambridge. Many years ago, students who were sent down were given a "mock funeral." The "body" was collected from the man's college and put into a hansom cab, and a procession went through the town to the railway station, with mourners in appropriate attire and a choir singing hymns. At the station the "body" was put into the guard's van.

A Boat Procession was formerly held on the day after the concluding day of the May Races, and crowds of about 10,000 people assembled on the lawn of King's College to see the decorated boats. The last Boat Procession was held in 1892, when the Lady Margaret eight was manned by only three men dressed in mourning. In the five empty seats were placards reading SENT DOWN. The missing men had been

12. Sent Down. "The Funeral" (H.A. Moden)

immediately rusticated for their part in a bonfire in New Court on the previous night.

XXI.   THE EMMANUEL COLLEGE INSURANCE SOCIETY

The Rt. Hon. Sir Geoffrey Shakespeare, in his memoirs *Let Candles Be Brought In,* describes how when he was "up" in 1920 he founded an Emmanuel Insurance Society to cover the risks of being "progged." For a premium of two shillings and sixpence an undergraduate would be reimbursed for any fine inflicted on him, and a premium of ten shillings covered a fine, a farewell dinner and a first class railway ticket to his home town if he should be sent down.

Canon C.E. Raven, who was then a Pro-Proctor and later Master of Christ's College and Vice-Chancellor, agreed to join his board of management. The Society flourished and surplus money was given to the college sports fund.

After an account of the Society appeared in a national newspaper, Shakespeare was summoned to appear before the Senior Proctor,

13. A Mock Funeral Procession in Hills Road

Dr T.R. Glover, who enquired how he dare treat the university regulations with contempt. "But, Sir, we expressly advise our members to obey the university regulations." "Nonsense, you encourage offenders by protecting them from the consequences of their offences." "I am sure Mr. Raven would never have joined our Board if such an interpretation could be put on our activities."

This placed Dr Glover in some difficulty, as he could not condemn Sir Geoffrey without censuring his colleague, so the interview ended by the imposition of a fine of £1, and the Insurance Society continued in business.

XXII.   THE PAVEMENT CLUB

A distinguished don said that it was the most surprising sight that he had ever seen. Hundreds of undergraduates sitting on the pavements and in the road at King's Parade. It happened at midday on a Saturday in 1921, and the occasion was the inaugural meeting of the Cambridge University Pavement Club.

Many undergraduates had previously received a notice to inform them that the object of the club was "to lend verisimilitude to the rapidly disappearing illusion that University life is a Life of Leisure." The Club's motto would be that "Sitting is the Seat of All Enjoyment" and the members proposed to sit, wind, weather and other circumstances permitting, upon the pavements of this ancient and honourable seat of learning at noon each fine Saturday of the Easter Term in pursuit of "entertainment, quiet conversation and the reading of newspapers aloud." The inaugural meeting would take place upon the pavement in King's Parade at noon, and a barrel organ recital and quiet games were to be the major attractions.

The barrel organ arrived at 11.50 a.m. and departed a few minutes later, escorted by the police. The members of the Club arrived in hundreds and sat down. Some had wisely brought cushions. They played cards, marbles, shove ha'penny and tiddly-winks.

The proceedings were interrupted by the arrival of the proctor and his bulldogs. Those nearest to him scrambled to their feet. Names were taken, the proctor passed on, and men sat down again. Then the proctor returned and the previous scenes were re-enacted.

A man appeared at a window and addressed the crowd which now numbered about two thousand. He thanked them for their attendance and forecast that the number of members would increase. If, next Saturday, King's Parade could not accommodate all of them, Market Hill would be used for an overflow meeting.

The proctor came back again, took more names and departed. Someone suggested that the club ought to elect a president. There were many cries of "The Proctor" and he was elected with acclamation. A proposal that the next meeting should take the form of a picnic lunch was adopted.

After singing, dancing, ring-a-roses and other diversions, someone rose to thank the audience and "the Cambridge Roberts, who, as usual, have been magnificent", and to declare the meeting closed. The crowd sang *Auld Lang Syne* and began to disperse.

A few days later, one of the organisers wrote to the press with reference to a discussion that he had had with the Proctor, C.F. Fay, "who behaved with such delightful fairness and leniency." He said that as an isolated rag it had been successful and welcome, but owing to the disruption of traffic it would not be possible to repeat it at the same place, because the police would have to take action and because some of the townspeople might feel offended. He pointed out that the organisers had anticipated that small groups would sit on the pavements, and had not foreseen the blocking of the road.

'In order to avoid offence to the public and the possible "sending down" of men chosen more or less at random, it was proposed to switch the picnic lunch to Parker's Piece.

Undoubtedly, the Pavement Club was one of the most novel and amusing of the Cambridge rags. It must have caused some anxiety to Mr R.J. Pearson, who had not long before been appointed Chief Constable, and the success of a number of organised rags in the following years was in a large measure due to his co-operation and forbearance.

XXIII.   SIR ARTHUR CONAN DOYLE FAILS TO MATERIALISE

In November 1921 hoardings in Cambridge displayed posters announcing that Sir Arthur Conan Doyle would lecture in the Guildhall on "Sex

14. Poppy Day, 1936 *(Cambridge Daily News)*

15. Poppy Day, 1936 *(Cambridge Daily News)*

Equality After Death" and would completely vindicate the theory of materialisation. At the time indicated the Guildhall was crowded, but the lecturer did not appear. Suddenly a white-robed figure came from the rear of the platform, bearing a banner inscribed with the words "Sir Arthur Conan Doyle Has Failed To Materialise." Pandemonium arose as the audience realised that it had been hoaxed.

XXIV. THE OPENING OF TOOT-AN-KUM-IN'S TOMB

The most spectacular rag of 1922 was the opening of the tomb of Toot-an-kum-in. The underground convenience on the Market Square, politely described by *The Times* as a "subway", served as the tomb, and after many preliminary events, such as the arrival of Cleopatra, the descent of "angels" on a rope from the Victoria Cinema, and fights by Egyptian soldiers, the tomb was entered. There were cheers as a variety of strange objects were handed out and displayed.

The most interesting object brought up was Phineas, the famous figure of a Highlander which for the previous ninety years had been the mascot of University College Hospital, London. It normally stood, secured by heavy chains, outside the premises of Messrs Catesby in Tottenham Court Road, and was only moved when it was needed by the Hospital to take part in a rag or a football match.

The capture of Phineas had been planned by undergraduates calling themselves the Caius Cooptimists who in November 1921 had captured a First World War German gun from Jesus College. Some time before the raid they visited Catesby's, ostensibly to purchase linoleum, and by chatting to the manager had discovered a great deal of useful information about Phineas.

On the 26th February, eleven men in a charabanc, one in a taxi and three in a car went to London, and a second party of twelve went by train. When they had all arrived, the taxi was parked just out of sight of the shop, and the charabanc a little further away.

At a pre-arranged signal, Catesby's doorway was secured, Phineas was unchained and bundled into the taxi which had drawn up at the right moment. Several men had previously located two or three policemen in the vicinity, and had told them that they were King's College (London) men who had been given permission to borrow Phineas for a rugby cup-tie that afternoon, so that when one of Catesby's assistants escaped from the shop and tried to raise the alarm, a policeman told him that it was all in order.

The mascot was quickly transferred from the taxi to the charabanc, which returned to Cambridge via Regent's Park and Golders Green, arriving by 2.30 p.m. Phineas was carried into Caius College through the Gate of Honour, and remained there until he was brought out of the "tomb". At the conclusion of the rag, he was returned to London by train.

XXV.   THE UNVEILING OF EROS BY KING HENRY VIII

This rag, which took place on the 9 March 1925, was an organized affair in aid of Addenbrooke's Hospital and the Cambridge Fruiting Campaign. The main event was the unveiling of a statue of Eros. A large triangular pedestal of scaffold poles and canvas was erected in the Market Place, but before the unveiling ceremony there were a great many other attractions, including an archery contest between the followers of Hengist and Horsa and those of Robin Hood, two genuine flower-sellers from Piccadilly; Ulysses, Nero, and hundreds of other strangely-attired characters.

Henry VIII arrived on a litter borne by Beefeaters, and was followed by Cardinal Wolsey in a scarlet gown. Just before the unveiling, an overcoat and a pair of trousers were lowered from the top of the pedestal.

The king pulled a rope, the canvas came down, and Eros was revealed. He proved to be a stalwart figure, O.M.H. Harmsworth of Pembroke College, who weighed eighteen stone. He was dressed in a red bathing costume and pink tights, with little white wings springing from his shoulders. The next event was a mannequin parade, and from among the maidens Henry VIII chose a seventh wife.

History was made on the following evening when the organisers of the rag dined in the Hall of Sidney Sussex College and had, as their principal guests, the Senior Proctor and the Chief Constable.

XXVI. THE OPENING OF JOANNA SOUTHCOTT'S BOX

This rag took place in 1927. A long procession of prelates included their lordships of Porwich, St. Alebuns and Pincoln, and the diminutive Bishop of Tichfield. The procession was held up at times by Bishop Stortford, but it finally reached the Market Square, where the Archbishops of Mutton and Pork opened Joanna Southcott's Box and produced from it a correct forecast of the Derby winner for that year.

XXVII. NIGHT CLIMBERS

For many years there were undergraduates who climbed university and college buildings during the night, and they had a guidebook called *The Night-Climbers of Cambridge,* also booklets about individual colleges.

From time to time, a variety of strange objects have appeared on the tops of buildings. On one occasion, two of the large statues high up on St. John's College Chapel were seen to be wearing surplices. A building firm was called in to remove them, and men erected a jib and a pulley on the summit of the tower, and lowered a workman on a rope.

While he was removing one of the surplices, a member of the college who was a well-known Alpine climber scaled the face of the tower and retrieved the other surplice.

One of the towers of the gateway of St. John's was once adorned by a bus stop sign which read "Bus Stop. Service 101. Head of Queue." On another occasion, female window-dressers' dummies appeared high up on Lloyd's Bank at the corner of Hobson Street and also on the Divinity School in St. John's Street.

§ Young, Geoffrey Winthrop, *The roof-climber's guide to Trinity, containing a practical description of all routes.* Cambridge, W.P. Spalding 1899.

Whipplesnaith (pseud.) *The Night Climbers of Cambridge.* London, Chatto and Windus, 1937.

The Night Climber's Guide to Trinity, 3rd edition, privately printed, 1960.

Hederatus (pseud.) *Cambridge Nightclimbing.* London, Chatto and Windus, 1970.

16. King's College Chapel during the invasion of Abyssinia *(Cambridge Daily News)*

17. A "Peace in Vietnam" banner on King's College Chapel. *(Cambridge Evening News)*

XXVIII.   CLIMBING KING'S COLLEGE CHAPEL

The corner towers of King's College Chapel have been climbed on many occasions. The climbers reached the roof by making use of a 'chimney' formed by a rib-buttress and a wall. By grasping a lightning conductor an inch in diameter, placing the feet against the rib-buttress and their back against the wall, they could make the slow and perilous ascent.

If one stands at the base of a tower, one can see spikes across the lower end of the traditional route, as well as at the base of the turrets, put there by the college to try to prevent these climbs.

In 1934, the feat was accomplished twice within a few days. On the first occasion, an umbrella was fixed to the top of a turret by two parties, each of three men. They said afterwards that each man took about fifteen minutes to reach the roof of the chapel, then, after two men had climbed up inside the turret to secure a rope to a beam and pass it down outside through the lattice-work, one man climbed to fix the umbrella. This took half an hour because the stone kept crumbling away.

Before the college authorities had called in steeplejacks to remove the umbrella, a Union Jack appeared on the north-east turret, and a flagon was suspended from a rope fixed between the pinnacle and the central cross. The flag appropriately celebrated Empire Day.

In 1936, when Mussolini's army invaded Ethiopia (then Abyssinia), a Union Jack and the Abyssinian flag were placed on the two turrets facing King's Parade, and between them was a large banner with the words SAVE ETHIOPIA.

One of the most spectacular climbs was accomplished during the night by three men who climbed to the roof of the chapel, then two went up to the top of the pinnacles. Across the fifty-foot gap they then fixed a banner, 38 feet long and 5 feet wide, with the words PEACE IN VIETNAM.

The domestic bursar of the college acknowledged that it had been "a very good climb. In the past we have had balloons, chamber pots and umbrellas on the pinnacles, but nothing like this."

One of the climbers said: "We must be anonymous, we don't want to be sent down. We were all highly experienced climbers but the journey up and down was terrifying. We decided to write immediately to the Dean of King's."

This letter said: "We would like to inform you on the basis of our experiences last night of the very dangerous condition of the stone-work on the pinnacles of your chapel. We suggest that unless restoration work is carried out immediately, the safety of future climbers of your chapel is in grave jeopardy."

XXIX. POPPY DAY

Undergraduate rags to raise funds for good causes are a feature of most universities, and for many years after the First World War a rag was

18. Poppy Day *(Cambridge Daily News)*

19. Poppy Day *(Varsity)*

20. Girton girls using punt-poles for crazy knitting during a 1976 rag *(Cambridge Evening News)*

held on "Poppy Day", the Saturday nearest to Armistice Day, to collect money for Earl Haig's Fund. Hundreds of students attired in a wide variety of costumes took part in innumerable stunts, some of them mounted on lorries which went in procession through the streets. There was usually a traction engine, and a battle of some kind on the river.

Some years ago, the students decided to donate the money collected to a number of good causes, the events taking place during the Lent Term. These changes were not popular with the public, and fewer undergraduates took part in them, but recently greater efforts have been made, and in 1977 about £10,000 was raised and divided between the Earl Haig Fund, Christian Aid, the Combined Cambridge Charities Organisation CARE, the Multiple Sclerosis Society and the Queen's Silver Jubilee Appeal.

21. One of the 22 beds on wheels which took part in a 12 mile race during the February 1977 rag *(Cambridge Evening News)*

Thirty-eight vehicles took part in a procession which caused traffic chaos for two hours, and throughout the city there were many amusing and novel stunts. Unfortunately, some of the participants pelted spectators with eggs, water and flour, and there were complaints from a number of townspeople. The Senior Proctor said "I had to walk through the crowd and saw a lot of Cambridge people whose patience seemed to be tried beyond measure" and he questioned whether "systematic hooliganism" had not affected the financial support given by the public.

Occasionally, undergraduate rags have had tragic consequences. A good-natured escapade by undergraduates after a dinner to celebrate the end of the 1977 Lent rowing races was followed by the death of a head porter. About twenty students attempted to lock the main gates of Clare College with a chain and padlock. Two porters successfully foiled the attempt, but one of them collapsed and died.

XXX.   THE BEST UNDERGRADUATE PRANK OF ALL TIME ?

Two undergraduate pranks were concerned with a car and a van. One night the porters of St. John's College heard some strange noises at about 3.0 a.m., but were not able to trace the source. At daybreak they discovered that an Austin car had been suspended below the Bridge of Sighs. It had been brought up the river during the night from Quayside on four punts.

An exploit hailed as the best student prank of all time took place in 1958. On the morning of Sunday 8 June, people walking along King's Parade were amazed to see that an Austin van had been placed on the roof of the Senate House, eighty-five feet above the ground.

How did it get there? The anonymous perpetrators of this feat claimed that they had dismantled some scaffolding being used on the Seeley Library, and had constructed a swinging derrick. Six men climbed to the roof of the Senate House, while others hauled on a rope running over a pulley. When the van had been raised to the roof, the derrick was dismantled and the scaffolding was replaced. They said that the whole operation had taken three hours and thirty-five minutes, and

22. The Austin van on the roof of the Senate House, 1958 *(Cambridge Daily News)*

that the most difficult moments had been when the van became wedged against a protruding part of the building when they had raised it about halfway.

When the van was examined, the exploit did not seem quite as extraordinary as had been thought, because it was found that the van must have been taken up in parts which had been bolted together at roof level. However, when two officials from the Home Office arrived in Cambridge on Tuesday, they urged the local Civil Defence men, as a matter of prestige, to lower it to the ground in one piece.

Ten men and a lorry arrived at 7.30 p.m. and rigged up a derrick it was found that it would not pass between the arms of the derrick, so it had to be dismantled and re-erected. At the second attempt, the tubular arms of the derrick began to buckle. The operations were being watched by a huge crowd, and students on the roof of Caius College offered much advice. One said: "You will have to get in a team of undergraduate contractors to do the job." By 9.30 p.m. it was clear that the Civil Defence men had been defeated, and that the van would have to be dismantled on the roof. They began to cut it up, and parts were lowered to the lorry in Senate House Passage. Work was resumed on Thursday evening, when the remainder of the van was cut up and lowered. By now it had taken much longer to get it down than to take it up, and the undergraduates had clearly won the greater prestige.